Let's Cl

The Misfit Kid

Ryan Hamilton

Copyright © 2017 by Ryan Hamilton

Thank you to all the readers who were here from the beginning, and to all those that are here now.

"We all have to realize there's something wrong in order to make a change."

"In order to have peace, we must find how to put all the pieces back together."

Why do we want to hate?

I have a dream

That one day

We won't race bait

To try and create hate.

Maybe one day

We will all awake

Maybe one day

We will learn

To not to divide

Maybe one day

We will rise up

And be there for one another.

Black or white

We are all the same

We are all running the same race

We shouldn't judge one another

By the color of one's face.

There's no reason

For all of this hate

Today

It's time for a change.

Be your own person

We see

What we are told to see

We believe

What we are told to believe

We are told to hate

When will we awake?

We have to change

We have to love one another

Doesn't matter

Rich or poor

Doesn't matter

Black or white

Doesn't matter

Man or woman

All that matters

Is treating someone

The way

You want to be treated.

We are all equal

We have

Different strengths

Different weaknesses

Don't let a weakness however

Derail you from

Showing the world your strengths

Be who

You were intended to become

Don't be

Who you are being told to be

Be

Who you want to be.

Changing the world

Isn't going to happen overnight

However

When that day comes

We all see the light

Everything will be alright.

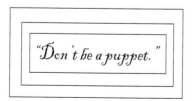

Just be nice

White

Black

Man

Woman

Rich

Poor

Straight

Gay

Transgender

None of it matters

If you're nice to me

Then guess what?

I'll be nice to you too.

The easiest thing

In the world to do

Is to just be nice

It seems hard to believe

But no one on this earth

Was born

To be mean

To be cruel

To not step up

And be a parent

To fight someone

For simply no reason

To destroy someone

From the inside

And out

That's not what this world

Is about.

This world

Is about being nice to people

Even if they aren't nice to you

Don't treat someone

How they treat you

Treat them

How you would treat

The one you love the most

Let them see

That this world

Isn't as cruel

As it's portrayed to be.

"You're making a difference when you can be nice to someone who isn't nice to you."

Picking each other up

We live in a world

Where people want to see

One another fail

We will step over anyone

Just to see our

Own selves succeed.

Why not pick up a brother

Or sister when they are down?

Don't kick them

While they are already on the ground

And no one else is around.

There are a little over 7 billion people on this earth

Each one of us

Has a story

Has a past

Has had a time where we feel no one cares

The worst feeling in the world

Is to feel as if

No one is in our corner

Be the person in the corner

That person on the ground needs

Pick them up

And let them see

That someone believes.

Us Men

Every day

Every night

There's tears rolling down

Millions of ladies faces because of us

And we ask for trust?

Maybe we should stop

Making our ladies cry so much.

Women cry and cry

But over and over

We don't care why

All we care about is making millions

We don't think we're men

If we actually show feelings.

It's horrible how we treat our ladies

Women aren't treated anywhere

Near how they should be

I really wouldn't want to see

What a woman has to see.

Us men have treated women wrong

For too long.

Women are beat up

Talked down to

And raped like it's nothing

Apparently

That's our way of showing loving

Instead

Let's show them loving

By helping them

To the best of our abilities

To become something

Because women have dreams too

If your girl wants to be a somebody in life

Don't deny her that right.

I really don't see how you'll put up with us

You'll deserve so much more

You're the ones

That go through nine months of hell

To have the babies

And then most of the time

We won't even step up

And be a father figure for our ladies.

It's a shame that to this day

Women are still just a man's "prize"

When are we going to learn that women deserve so much more than just putting up with our lies?

Why do women deserve to be treated like possessions?

Why do women deserve to be left to raise a baby on their own?

Why do women deserve to be beat up?

Why do women deserve to be raped?

Why do women deserve to be killed?

That's right

They don't deserve that at all

What us men need to do

Is build our women up

And make them stand tall

Because in this world

It's so easy to be knocked down and fall.

Love through the eyes and mind of The Misfit Kid.

The man in the chair

As I walk down the street

I see him

The old man in the chair

He's reminiscing on

What life once was

While the misfit kid

Is dreaming about what life could be.

Fast forward a few years

And the old man's time

Is running down

One of these days

He won't be around

Did he do all he wanted?

Did he make a sound?

I want to make a sound

And I know to make it

I have to fully understand love.

Fast forward a few more years

And the misfit kid

Is the one having the kid

Now

He gets to see what it means to live.

Love comes down to three main things when it comes to relationships:

You have to love each other like you're 100

Make love like you're 23

Play around like you're 13

Show the world

That you believe

Show the world

That love is the best thing

In this world you can receive.

Here's how I view everything about love.

First sight

Can you fall in love at first sight?

Can just one look find Mr. or Miss Right?

Maybe

Maybe not.

I've heard the stories

He or she fell in love by first glance

And was forever put in a trance.

Maybe it's possible

Maybe it's not

But

If everything is based on looks

Then it can't be love

Because

How do you know how their personality is?

How do you know how they treat others?

How do you know how they are behind closed doors?

You don't know

You can't be in love by attraction alone.

Maybe in movies

And the fairytale world

But in the real world

Love involves getting to know each other

It takes being there for one another

Through the good

And the bad.

"We are in a world where we try to make things happen overnight."

The first few months

Everything at first

Is complete perfection

You're happy

They're happy

You think they're the best

Different from the rest

In your mind

There won't be a next.

Unfortunately

This is just the honeymoon stage

A stage where we all wish

We could stay in forever.

Once the honeymoon wears off

Things change

And most of the time

For the worse.

You realize something

They're different than your ex

But not really

They have their flaws

Not like him or her

But you realize they're not perfect like you thought they were.

The first few months are like no other

It seems like you'll will be together forever.

The passion is as if you're in another world

You don't want to leave their side

For those first few months

You'll are each other's ride or die.

The happiest time of most relationships

Is the first few months

Then there is no more "love."

Lust and Love

The difference

Between lusting

And loving someone is

The difference between night and day.

Lust is just a physical attraction

Love is a one of a kind connection.

Every day

People think they "love" someone

When really they are just lusting after them

If the best thing you like about them

Is the sex

Then let them be with someone else.

Don't lead someone on

Just because of lust

Letting go is a must.

"We live in a generation where lusting with ten people is more popular than being in love with one."

Burning passion

Early on

You will know

It won't take long

For you to know

If they're

The one

Your heart

Will know

Before your mind does.

If your heart doesn't

Burn for them

Then you simply

Don't love them.

When you're in love

Your heart

Burns for them

From first kiss

To the first fight

They make your

Heart happy

And they make

Your heart sad.

But you'll know

Because sometimes

You'll feel as if

They set your heart

On fire.

You'll really know

When your heart

Beats out of your chest

When you fight

Because

It'll be

The same result every time

You hate them

But love them the next very second

It's all because of the

Burning passion

The passion that will

Hurt you

Pick you back up

Hurt you

And pick you up again.

Looks

It doesn't matter
What someone looks like
If you love them…
Then you love them.

Of course
You have to be physically
Attracted to them
But looks
Really don't mean much
If they do
Then just stick with lust.

If all you care about is looks
Then love isn't for you
Love is about much more
Than how they look.

I don't care if they're fat
And you're skinny
I don't care if they're black
And you're white
I don't care if they're a man
And you're a man
I don't care if they're a woman
And you're a woman

People are going to judge you

No matter what

It doesn't matter what they think

People judge relationships

Based on how you'll

Look together

It doesn't matter

How you'll look together

What matters is that

If you're happy

And he/she is happy too

What matters is how

You treat them

And how

You treat them too.

Looks don't matter

As much as the world

Want us to believe

That they do

Of course

They're good to have

But when it comes to

Real love

They really don't

Mean much

It might sound simple

But it's true

All that matters is

How in your heart

You really feel

About them.

Treat them the same

I don't care if

You're around your friends

I don't care if

You're around your family

Don't disrespect

Your boyfriend/girlfriend

To just be "cool."

No matter

Who you're around

Always

And always

Treat them the same

Don't play around

With them

Like some sick game.

More times

Than not

The relationship

Is different

When you'll

Are around somebody else

You feel like

A prince/princess

When you'll are alone

But you feel like

A stranger

When you'll aren't.

It's simple

If they only treat you good

When it's convenient

For them

Then guess what?

They don't love you.

Treat them

How you want to be treated

I don't care

Who you'll are around

I don't care

Who you're trying to impress

Because

They should be the only one

You're trying to impress

So

No matter who you'll are around

Make them feel like

The luckiest

Man/woman in the world.

First love

There's nothing else like it

Your first love

Will change you forever

A part of you will never be the same.

Some of us get lucky

For some

The first love will be who they end up saying "I do"

For everyone else

They will have to watch their first love with someone new.

The first love is the most interesting

They will change how you view the world

How you trust people

And how you will love again.

When you love for the first time

You're not afraid of anything

You put them before anyone else

It's almost as if

You breathe the air they breathe.

You're comfortable around them

They became not only your boyfriend/girlfriend

But also your best friend.

First love is the

Best

Worst

Happiest

And saddest

All at the same time.

"A first love can turn you into the person that you will be for the rest of your life. You have to combine the good/bad and improve yourself regardless of how the relationship turns out."

When you know

How do you know when you're in love?

Going from really liking someone

To "being in love"

Is the biggest step.

When you put them

Before your own self

Then you know

You know you've found it

You've found the thing

That is about to take you on

A never-ending rollercoaster.

When it hurts just seeing them talk to another guy/girl

Then you know

When it hurts being away from them

Then you know

When you're happy because they're happy

Then you know

When you're mad because they're mad

Then you know.

When you're bored

The first few months are perfect

You can't get enough of each other

You dress up for them

You laugh at all their jokes

You simply don't want to disappoint them.

Everything they say is marvelous

The way they smile

The way they kiss

The way they hug

In your mind

You wish those months could forever be on rewind.

The passion can only last so long

So when all the puppy dog love is over

And you find out

Who they really are

What will you do?

When you get bored

Will you just leave?

Or will you stay?

And love them for forever

And a day.

You really find out if you love someone

When you get bored

The fire is gone

But that doesn't mean it has to be over.

The first part of the relationship is special

But the next step is just as amazing

Growing together is

What it is all about

Love is about staying together

Even when you're bored.

As time goes on

Your heart won't beat as fast when you see him/her

That doesn't mean you don't love them

What that means is you've reached the next step

The step where you have to

Make the decision

Stay and see if you'll can make it to the next step

Or go and do it all over again

With someone new.

Steps

Love is all about the next step

Only two things can happen in a relationship

Either you keep on moving

To the next step

Or your love will fail

And be like the rest.

Love is about trying to make it

To the top of the steps

To the place where

We all want to be

A place you can't see

The destination of happiness.

The final step is to be

Happily in love

To really have it all

And not let it fall

Is like

Jumping over a fence fifty foot tall.

Climbing these steps

Is the hardest climb you'll make

But it's worth it

Because if you don't take the leap

Then you'll regret it

You'll know

You should have tried

Instead of letting go.

Life without love

What is life without love?

A life of no feelings

A life without a care in the world

Just stress free

And becoming everything

You dreamed you would be.

It sounds perfect

But it really isn't

Does love hurt?

Of course

It can be constant stress

It can make you do things

You never thought you would do

It'll make your heart stop

Make your heart feel like it's on fire

But it's all worth it

Love is worth the pain

The hate

The crying

The what you think is

A complete waste of time.

Nobody ever said love would be easy

It'll take work

They'll mess up

And you'll mess up too

But that's no excuse to move on to someone new.

What is life without love?

It's a life of not taking chances

A life of what will be regret

For not finding "the one"

A life of only self-goals

No goals of a family

Because of a few times being hurt.

You can't let one or two people

Hurt your future happiness

We all will have a broken heart

But you can't let that rip you apart.

If you get knocked down

You have to get back up

Don't let temporary hurt

Bring you down forever

There's seven billion people in the world

Get back up

And keep on loving

Keep on trying to find love

Because life without it

Is a life

That might not be complete.

When it comes to relationships

You can be happy

Without love

But more times than not

Life is much better

With love.

"You don't have to be in a relationship to complete any life fulfillment goal. You can be happy without being in a relationship. But you can't be happy without love completely."

Loving two people

In my opinion

One of the most interesting topics of love

Is if you can love two people

At the same time

Is it possible?

Is it a real thing to love two people at the same time?

No

It's not possible

You don't love either one of them

If you think you do.

When you love someone

All you think about is them

If you're doing the same thing

With someone else

You don't deserve either person

Because loving someone

Doesn't involve having the same exact feelings

For the other person too

If love is like that

From your point of view

Then you don't need to be saying

The words "I love you."

You can love multiple people

In your lifetime

But two people at the same time?

No it isn't possible.

Deserve you

Just because you love someone

Doesn't mean

Abuse

Physically

Emotionally

Or mentally is okay

I don't care what they say

They don't deserve to have you

Every day.

Who abuses the one they love?

Exactly

That isn't love

In their eyes

You're a possession

Love has nothing to do with it

You have to realize

The "I love you" they say is a lie

They don't deserve you

And they know they don't.

For some reason

Being treated horrible

Is what some people like

I hate to say it

But in most instances

The ones who deserve you
You take advantage of
The ones who don't deserve you
You stay with
The good guy/girl doesn't win much
More people would rather have lust
They'd rather have temporary happiness
Than something that
Will last forever.

Be with the person that deserves you
And you deserve them
It's simple
Be with the one that treats you like
A king
Or a queen
Not the one that treats you
As a toy.

Cheating

You cheat

They cheat

You say "I love you"

They say "I love you too"

I'm not sure when cheating on someone

Became a way to show

How you much you love them.

They say "I'm sorry"

You take them right back

Some people cheat

To get back even

But the thing is

The score will never be even

Once someone cheats

Then the game is on

They cheat

You cheat

They cheat again

You cheat again

The score is technically "even"

But is it really?

Cheating

Doesn't solve anything

You say you "forgive them"

They say they "forgive you"

But you know they don't

And you know you don't.

Can you cheat and still love someone?

Well of course

Everyone makes mistakes

Nobody is perfect

But making the same mistake

Over

And over again

Is not love

I know relationships that ended up working

After someone cheated

But I know more relationships that didn't work

After someone cheated

In no circumstances

Is cheating ever a good thing

It ends up leading to the

"I hate you"

And "I hate you too."

"Karma always will come back. If you're unfaithful, then don't be mad when someone is unfaithful to you. If you're faithful, you will eventually be with the one that deserves you."

Forgiving

Forgiveness

By far one of the hardest things to do

It's easy to say we forgive someone

We can say anything

Without actually meaning it.

The hardest time to forgive though

Is when it comes to love

When it comes too

The lying

The cheating

When do you forgive?

When do you not?

One can only take so much

There's a time when enough

Is enough.

You can only say "sorry" so many times

Eventually

It becomes impossible

To forgive them anymore

Every time they mess up

You start to love them

A little bit less

They become just like the rest.

You can't let your forgiveness

Be taken advantage of

Not even if it's the one

You love.

Forgiveness in a relationship

Is key

Although

If you have to forgive

Over and over

They aren't worth it

You need to move on.

Temptations

Love is never easy

The truth of it is

More people want you

When you're taken

Some people get the thrill

Of messing relationships up

Some people don't care about love.

It doesn't matter who you are

You're going to get tempted

It won't be easy saying no

But if you say yes

You'll regret it

When you get tempted

You have to remember

That one day of fun

Isn't worth losing a lifetime of happiness.

The worst time to be tempted

Is when you're mad

Your boyfriend/girlfriend

And you are having an argument

They say something

You say something

Then before you know it

You messed up

And things will never

Be the same

You fell for the game.

You can't be afraid

Love can be tough

You might end up

Having heartbreak

After heartbreak

But you can't be afraid

You have to continue to love

Because love can also be

The most beautiful thing in the world.

There's plenty of reasons

To be afraid

I understand that

But you can't miss out

On who is "your meant to be"

Because you didn't open your eyes

To see.

Love can be perfect

It can let you see

How much your heart

Can drop

And then

Beat fast in the same minute.

You view life differently

When you're in love

Caring for someone

Can make you want

To do better as a person

You'll want to do

Whatever it takes

To make him/her happy

Because love

Can make you do anything.

You can't be afraid

Let someone

Fix your broken heart

Because

You truly never know

When you'll find

Your "forever."

Climax

Every relationship runs into it

Things aren't as exciting

You don't want to be around them

24/7

The passion isn't as high

You can no longer see

The same look in their eyes

Because

The climax has arrived.

The puppy dog part of

The love is gone

That doesn't mean it's time

To move on

Not at all

That's the problem

With most relationships

These days

When things get dull

People move on.

Once upon a time

Things were way different

There was a time

Where love meant something

Today it means nothing

When it's not fun

Or convenient for someone anymore

They leave.

We live in a generation

Where we only love

Until it gets to the climax.

"At some point, things will reach a peak where you have to decide
what you want in life. Do you just want to have temporary fun? Or do
you want to make it work through the climax and make it last forever?"

Jealousy

The ugliest part of love

Is when it comes to jealousy

You don't want to see

Them around anyone

You've became over-protective

This can be a

Good and

Bad thing

It just depends on how bad

It gets.

There's nothing wrong

With being jealous

It just means that you care

But sometimes

It makes you unaware.

Jealousy can turn you

Into a different person

Honestly

If you let it

It'll turn you into

A monster

It'll turn you into

Someone you don't even recognize

When you look in the mirror.

Jealousy can eat you alive

Every word that's comes out of their mouth

You think is a lie

Not because they did anything

But because

Jealousy has made you

Look at them different

Everything different

You don't trust

Anyone

In your mind

Everyone is the enemy

In reality

You don't even

Love him/her anymore

They've became more

Of a possession

Than a boyfriend/girlfriend

When someone talks to them

You feel as if

They are literally

Trying to steal from you.

Drug

I look at loving someone

As a drug

You need them

You want them

You have to have them.

They aren't good for you

But also they are

They make you feel

Good

Bad

Mad

And sad

All at the same time sometimes.

Sometimes

You can't get enough

Other times

You want to leave them alone.

They can't get out of your head

You've became addicted

Inside

And out

You're hurting

You want it to stop

But then again

You want the feeling to last forever.

People tell you

To leave them alone

You deserve better

You deserve the world

You deserve perfection

That's not what you want though

You want him/her

You want the drug

You want the imperfection

The thing that hurts you

But makes you

Feel perfect at the same time

The one you call "mine."

The imperfection

A lot of relationships

Have problems when

Things are going wrong

When the relationship

Is heading down

People don't stick around.

No relationship is perfect

Basically

Because two imperfect people

In a relationship

Will result

In arguments

Fights over nothing

Tears

Regret

Pain

It's all part of the game.

The game of love

Is a game like no other

A lot of times

You're wondering why

You're playing

At the same time though

You know the imperfection

Is worth it in the end.

Nobody looks perfect

Nobody acts perfect

Nobody always does the right thing

Guess what though?

That's the beauty of

What we call love

The imperfection of relationships

Can lead to the

Years of laughter

And the happily ever after.

The past

The man/woman you were before

The things you did wrong

It doesn't matter if it was

The constant lying

The constant cheating

The constant feeling of

"Never being good enough"

The past

Is the past

Put it behind you fast

Because if you don't

Your future relationships

Won't last.

The past means nothing

But it also

Means everything

It's all up to you

Are you going to move on?

Or will you let the past eat you alive?

If you let it

The past will hurt you forever

Your relationships with friends

Family

And most definitely

With the guy/girl you love.

The past

Makes you who you are today

Tomorrow

And the person you'll be

For the rest of your life

Some people really

Never move on

They let the past

Take them over

They let that boy/girl

From years ago

That hurt them

Control their future happiness.

If you don't let go

Then you'll never know

You'll never know

The "What could you have been?"

Because you were too busy

Trying to think

And make right of something

That you can't control

What has been already done

Cannot be taken back

You made a mistake

Or they made a mistake

It doesn't matter

Move on from the past

Because if you don't

You might end up

Missing out on who

You were meant to be with.

Love has a lot

To do with the past

It's all up to you

Do you want to be who you were yesterday?

Or who you could become tomorrow?

"We can't change the past. But we can repeat it over and over again."

Who you were before

You know the type of relationship

The type where

They always bring up

The man/woman you were before

The one that isn't like

The one you are today.

Some people

Will always remember you

For who you were before

It doesn't matter

If you turn your life around

And become

The most successful person there is

Through some people's eyes

You're the same person

You were five

Or ten years ago.

It's the same thing with relationships

They bring up a mistake you made

Before you even met them

It shouldn't matter

But for some reason

It does.

If that's how they feel

Then that's not love

When you love someone

You don't care

Who they were before.

Most of us

Won't go through life

Without messing up

We'll make mistakes

We'll care about the ones

That don't care about us

And we'll not care about

The ones that care about us.

That's life

We sometimes learn more

From the ones

That messed us over

Than the ones

That loved us

With everything they had.

We don't think about it

But love

Is all about

Who we were before

If it wasn't for being

Lied too

Cheated on

Betrayed

Over and over again

Then we wouldn't know

How to really love.

There's nothing wrong

With who you were before

Because without that person

Then you would never

Learn how to love the one

That'll you be forever saying

"I love you" too.

Love makes you weak

Let's make no mistake

Love can be

The best thing that'll ever happen to us

But the truth of it is…

Love makes you weak.

Before we fall in love

Our dreams

Are to travel

And explore the world

As kids

We have so many dreams

We look into the sky

Thinking no one will ever hurt us

Thinking we can save the world

Thinking we can live forever.

Then comes love

The thing that can single-handily

Destroy every dream

We've ever had

The first time you fall in love

You feel as if

You're on top of the world

You just want to run around

And sing

You can't wait to give or

Be given that

"One of a kind diamond ring."

Unfortunately

Most of the time

Things don't run that smoothly

Before you know it

Your heart has been

Shattered into a million pieces

The world doesn't look

Like it once did

Your dreams

Don't look like they once did

All because

Of the thing we call "Love."

You see...

Even if your first love is "the one"

That doesn't mean you're still

Not weak

Once you fall in love

Your mind will never

Be able to imagine

The things

That it could once imagine.

Every day you fall

More and more in love

The more and more

Weaker you get

Love is amazing

But love makes you weak.

Can't help who you love

It doesn't matter

What anybody else thinks

It doesn't matter

What makes you popular

It doesn't matter

What the color of their skin is

It doesn't matter

What gender they are

You love who you love

Who cares what they think

You can't help who you love.

Love is beautiful

It's truly

A one of a kind sight

You can see

When two people love each other

From miles away

Just the way

They look at each other

Just the way

They smile at each other

Just the way

They light up when they're together

It's the type of feeling

We all want forever.

When you love someone

Be proud of them

Show them off

Let the whole world know

How happy they make you

Don't be afraid

Because

You can't help who you love

You love them

And they love you

And guess what?

That's all that matters.

When they're gone

Love is all about

Finding out how much you care

When they're gone

When they've moved on

And you're standing still

Wondering why

You let them

Walk out the door.

You took them for granted

You treated them like

They would always be there

You never thought about

What if they leave?

What if they finally have had enough?

Out of nowhere

They're gone

And they're not coming back.

You have to love them

When they're there

People

Aren't going to stick around forever

If you don't treat them

How they deserve to be treated

Then why should they stay?

They deserve the one

That treats them

Like a king

Or a queen

Not the one

That treats them like trash

On the street.

Sometimes

It takes losing them

To know how much

You really loved them

By then though

It might be too late

Their heart might beat

For someone else

Someone new

Someone

That loves them

Better than you

Someone

That respects them

Loves them for

Who they are

Not for

What they do for them.

They love you

When you don't love them

Then when you

Decide to love them

Then they don't love you

Sometimes

That's just how love goes

So don't take advantage

Of their heart

Because when they're gone

You'll realize

He/she was more

Than good enough.

"Don't wait until they're long and gone… to figure out that you let the love of your life walk out the door."

50/50

Love takes both sides

In order to work

It can't be

100/0

90/10

80/20

70/30

60/40

It has to be

50/50

You have to try

As much as they are

Or

They have to try

As much as you are.

If it isn't

50/50

I can promise you

It won't work

Both of you

Have to fight through the

Arguments

It doesn't matter if

The argument is over

Something little

Or

Something serious

You'll can't give up

Always

Meet halfway.

It's simple

When it comes down to it

If both of you

Put the 50/50 in

The relationship will work

If you'll don't

Then the relationship won't work.

Love can be

I've talked a lot about

The things that can

Go wrong with love

But love can be

The best thing there is

In the world

It's all up to you

Love is what

You make it to be

Let it be something

That you want to see.

If you let it...

Love can be

Perfection

From the first time you'll meet

To the first date

To the first kiss

To the seeing each other 24/7

To the falling in love

Love can be

A beautiful ride

A ride where

If you let it...

They'll forever be by your side.

There is

No other feeling

To your lips

Wanting to kiss them forever

To your hugs

Never wanting to let them go

To your heart

Beating out of your chest

To your mind

Constantly thinking about them

Love can simply be

A beautiful thing.

You will never find anything

To compete with love

Love is

The greatest thing this world

Has to offer

If you let it…

Love can be the thing

That makes you

A better person

Love can be the thing

That turns you

Into the person

You were intended to become.

Everything is better

The singe life can be fun

But it's not the same

Everything is better

When you're in a relationship

Where you'll love each other

When you're single

And you kiss someone

It means nothing

When you'll sleep together

It means nothing

Without love

It means nothing

With love

It means everything

Everything you'll do

Even if it's just going out

To the movies

Means absolutely everything.

You try to make yourself

Believe you're happy

But you know you're not

Because you know

Everything is better

With love

Going out to eat

Going on vacation

Going to sleep

It's all better

With someone you love.

There's nothing

That can replace love

You'll try

To find another source

But there isn't one

Love is the answer

It might sounds crazy

But it's the answer

To everything.

You're unhappy

You're fed up

You just don't understand

You want to be happy

But you don't want to be

In a relationship

Because he/she made you

Never want to love again

I understand

But you have to understand too

Everything is better

With love

Happiness

Is found when you love

The answer to making your

Life complete

Comes when you

Find love.

"Life is much simpler when you settle down."

Being young

I hear all the time

That someone young

Doesn't know

What love is

Is there a certain age you know what love is?

Of course not

Someone at sixteen

Can know more about love

Than someone at fifty six

Being young has

Nothing to do with it.

Some of us fall in love

For our first time

At sixteen

Others

Won't find it

Until later on

Just because you didn't

Love at sixteen

Doesn't mean that you

Can tell someone

It is impossible

Because it's not

There's no such thing

As an

Age limit to love.

Sometimes

The best love stories

Come when you're young

Being young

And in love

Is one of the

Best and worst

Feelings in the world.

You can grow up

Very fast

If you have your first heartbreak

When you're young

You'll learn that

You can't trust people

Like you thought you could

At the same time though

If your young love

Lasts forever

Then you'll be able to

Grow through your

Teenage years

Young adult years

Middle aged years

And old years

All with the same person

What would we better than that?

It really doesn't matter

What people think

If you're in love

You'll know it

Being young

Or being old

It really doesn't matter

The feeling will be the same

No matter what age you are.

Your heart

Your mind

Your eyes

Your smile

All work in a different way

It's hard to really

Put into words

But love

Makes you

A different person.

Being young

And in love

Will make you

The happiest

You've ever been

And the most mad

You've ever been.

Love is love

Let your heart love

No matter what age you are.

Let's be real

Our generation

Is all about

Ourselves

We could care less

About love

Let's be real

This isn't fifty

Eighty

Or a hundred years ago.

Once upon a time

Love meant something

There was rarely ever

A divorce

Today

Divorce happens

Without anyone blinking an eye.

Love stories are a

Dying breed

The being together for

Fifty

Sixty

Seventy years

Let's be real

The way things are going

People will have to have a

Parade at twenty years.

Cheating

Lying

Leaving your family

It isn't viewed

Like it once was

It's horrible

But it's true

The only thing

We love

Is the one that's

Staring back at us

In the mirror

Once it becomes inconvenient…

We run

And look for the

Next good time.

Love?

This is a generation

Without love

The dreams

Of having a family

Of having a husband/wife

For a lifetime

Isn't a dream for people
Anymore.

Let's be real
The divorce rate
Is currently at fifty percent
If nothing changes
It'll be at
Sixty percent
Seventy percent
Eighty percent
Ninety percent
Before we blink.

Love becomes more
Than just about you
And him/her
When you'll have kids
And you decide to leave
If you really think you're
The only one affected
Then you need to be lectured
When you leave
Without thinking
You're just not
Leaving him/her
You're leaving your kids too.

Love is about much more

Than relationships

It's about friendships

It's about how

You treat your mother/father

It's about how

You treat your son/daughter

Let's be real

Love isn't about

What you do in front

Of everyone

It's about

What you do behind the scenes

It's about

What you do when

No one is looking

When the lights are off

What type of son/daughter are you?

What type of friend are you?

What type of father/mother are you?

What type of boyfriend/girlfriend are you?

Mystery

Love is a complete…

Mystery

There's no such thing as

Perfecting the art

Of love

You have to realize

That love

Will throw curveballs

When you least

Expect it

You think you know

Someone

When in reality

You didn't know

They were

A stranger

Dressed up like

A friend

A boyfriend/girlfriend

A husband/wife

Some people

Live a different life.

On the other side

You might fall in love

With someone

You never thought you would

The one

You called your best friend

Just six months ago

Has now become

The one you're going to

Say "I do" too.

Love is

Just how life is

One day

You feel as if

You're the happiest man/woman

In the world

Then

The very next day

You'll feel as if you're the saddest.

Love is something

That will throw you down

And pick you

Right back up

You just have to realize that…

Love is a mystery.

Lessons

Just like life

Love is all about

Lessons

There's a reason

We get cheated on

Or cheat on someone

We lie to someone

Or they lie to us

We lose their trust

Or they lose our trust.

It's all a lesson

From first connection

To first impression

To first depression

It's all okay

Because it's all a lesson

At the end of the day.

Just like life

You'll either learn

From your lesson

Or

You'll do it again

Some people

Will cheat

And lie

Over and over again

Wondering why

They're not happy

They'll blame

Everyone

Except the one

That is to blame

The one

Playing the game.

Cheating

And lying will never

Lead to forever happiness

It's only temporary

Until he/she learns

That you're not worth it

In reality

You're only cheating

And lying to yourself

Why cheat on someone that doesn't cheat on you?

Why lie to someone that doesn't lie to you?

Because

We don't care about

The ones that care about us

We care about

The ones that don't

We would rather

Just "have fun"

Instead of forever

"Being in love."

You have to learn

From your lessons

I don't believe in the…

"Once a cheater

Always a cheater"

People can change

But that's up to you

It's nobody else's choice

You either

Learn from your lessons

Or you don't.

"Life is love. Love is life. We're taught how to become the person we become from bad relationships, good relationships, and the one relationship that lasts forever."

Regrets

The

"What could have been"

The

"What would have been"

When it comes to love

In no circumstances

Do you ever want

To have regrets

The

"One you shouldn't have let go"

The

"One you cheated on"

The

"One you never said I love you"

The list goes on

Every day

People regret

Letting the one they truly loved

Go.

Love is about

The decisions we make

The decision

To listen to your heart

Or not

The decision

To not speak up

When you should have

There's nothing worse

Than watching

The one you love

With someone else.

When you're in a relationship

With someone

You don't really love

When they're in a relationship

With someone they

Don't really love

Then all you have

Is regrets

Don't let that be you

Do whatever it takes

If your best

Isn't good enough

Then you can live with that

But if you don't try

Then you'll live

The rest of your life

Knowing that could have

Your husband/wife.

The best love

Whether we admit it

Or not

All of us want it

We want the love

That last

Fifty

Sixty

Seventy years

We want the best love

We want the life

With the one

We truly love

It doesn't matter

Who you are

Deep down

It's what you want

You don't want

The "perfect" love

You want the one

That is with the one

You were destined

To spend forever with.

The best love

Isn't about perfection

It's about

Making it work

Through the fights

Making it work

When you're bored

Making it work

When they mess up

Making it work

When you mess up

Making it work

When nobody else

Thinks you'll can

Be each other's

Number one fan.

The best love

Is sometimes

The one that no one

Doesn't know much about

The world doesn't have

To know

Everything you'll do

When you're "in love"

You could care less

About

What anyone thinks

All you care about

Is the one

You want to spend

Forever

And eternity with.

So what is it?

What is love?

One of the most interesting questions

In the world by far

It makes you

Have a different smile

It makes you

Have different tears

It makes you

A better person

It makes you

A worse person.

Love is

The best thing

You'll ever come across

Love is

The worst thing

You'll ever come across.

Love makes you

Learn about yourself

It makes you

Learn about the world

It makes you

Into this person

You never thought

You would become

Sometimes

For the better

Sometimes

For the worse

Love is

The thing

That makes us

Turn things around

In our life

Or it makes

Our life go downhill.

Love can make you

Hate

If you were

Cheated on

And lied too

Continuously

Then love can

Make you not trust

Love can make

You never want to love again.

Love can

Turn you from a boy/girl

To a man/woman

The decisions you make

From love

Can make you

Grow up overnight.

You'll see

That how you love

Your boyfriend/girlfriend

Husband/wife

Will transfer over

To how you

Treat your

Best friend

Your mother/father

Your son/daughter.

Love others

The same way

You want to be loved

Just be faithful

Just be truthful

Just be there

Love

Love

And love again.

Love your

Boyfriend/girlfriend

Husband/wife

Best friend

Mother/father

Son/daughter

With everything in you

We only get

One chance at life

Make your one time

Here memorable

Make your one time

With no regrets

Make your one time

As an example

Be a role model

Set the standard

To love others

How you want the ones

After you to love.

"What is love? Love is about what you make it to be."

Sincerely,

The Misfit Kid

Men and Women

You can't put down

A whole gender

Just because of

One man

Or one woman

There are good men

There are good women

There are bad men

There are bad women.

In relationships

There are men that are faithful

However

There are men that cheat

Same thing goes for women

There are women that are faithful

There are women that cheat.

Don't force yourself not to love

Just because of one man/woman

Trying to protect yourself like that

Will impact

Other parts of your life

Let it go

And everything

Will be alright.

Before you can help

Change the world

You must do

Whatever it takes

To help yourself

Love

Let everything be

Open your eyes

And see

That men and women

Are the same

Some are good

Some are bad

It's as simple as that

Well at least

That's what I believe.

Blessing or a Lesson

I'm a firm believer in

Everyone

We meet on this earth

Is for a blessing

Or a lesson.

Whether it's a

Boyfriend/Girlfriend

A friend

Or family

We are all

Going to run into lessons

We find a good man/woman

A good friend

And family we can trust

All from the mistakes

We made by

A certain relationship with someone.

Those lessons

Turn into a blessing

The wrong relationships

Teach us

What to look for

To find a good relationship.

We have to change our outlook

On when we say

We wish we never met a

Certain someone

Because without meeting that man/woman

You wouldn't know

How to go stronger

And realize

What you are looking for

In a friend

Or

In a boyfriend/girlfriend.

Don't judge

Doesn't matter

What family you come from

Doesn't matter

How much money you have

Doesn't matter

How popular you are

Never look down on another man.

Don't judge

Just love.

Let it be known

That all the money you have

Can be taken away at any time

Show good character

Show that you care

Be aware

People will struggle

Addiction of any kind

Can take someone to another place

But don't judge

Just love.

I've said it before

And I'll say it again

Help someone get back up

Don't just leave them lying on the floor

Don't judge just because

Someone looks different

Or acts different

We're all different for a reason

Embrace the uniqueness

There is in each individual.

You might be

Somewhere better today

But just remember

They could be in a better place tomorrow.

Don't judge

Just love.

"Don't judge unless you can magically walk a day in another man's shoes."

Be thankful

You can see

You can hear

You can talk

You can walk

Be thankful

Because not everyone can.

You have food

You have water

You have a roof over your head

You have a car

Be thankful

Because not everyone does.

You have a father

You have a mother

You have a brother

You have a sister

Be thankful

Because not everyone

Is as lucky as you.

You have a bad job

Be thankful that you have one.

You don't need to have the

Newest shoes

Newest clothes

Be thankful

For everything that you do have.

You woke up this morning

Be thankful you're still here.

You are not defined

You don't have to be

Who you were last year

Last month

Or even yesterday

Today is a new day.

Change who you surround yourself around

Change how you treat people

Become the man/woman

You were intended to become

It's never too late

To flip the page.

You are not defined

By who you were yesterday

Change who you are today

You can't help

Change the world

Until you change yourself.

Do not be defined

By your mistakes

Become a role model

Become a leader

Become someone

Who can truly say

You are not defined by who

You were yesterday

Today is a new day.

We are one world

Africa

Antarctica

Asia

Australia

Europe

North America

South America

Seven continents

All different places

All different faces.

Different languages

Different religions

Different styles of living

But guess what?

We are all one world

Care about everyone

Care about making this world

A better world.

We are currently

In the year 2016

There should no longer

Be segregation.

It's time for unity

The biggest issue

In the United States currently

Is a

Black lives matter

Blue lives matter divide

The truth of it is

Both lives matter

All lives matter.

Never let someone tell you

One life

Means more than another

We are told

To not have peace

We are told

To hate and disrespect

Without thinking about

What we know is best.

The best thing that we can do

Is love everyone

Regardless of ethnicity

Don't let hatred

Destroy lives

Let's change the world

Let's all rise.

"We all have a place in this world."

We are together

Just because

They believe differently

And live life differently

Doesn't mean you live better

There's no such thing

As a lesser person.

Some men love women

Some men love other men

Some women love men

Some women love other women

You don't have to accept

The lifestyle they choose to live

Because guess what?

The lifestyle they live

Is not your life.

You don't have to belittle someone

Just because

They don't see

How you see

Everyone is different

We all don't

Suppose to be alike

We all

Suppose to view the world

With a different perspective

But no matter

What you believe

And no matter

How you live

We can all

Show each other

Some respect

And

Change this world together.

Care like you should

Being a good son/daughter

Being a good father/mother

Being a good friend

Being a good boyfriend/girlfriend

All things

That should seem like good traits

However

We live in a generation

Where people take advantage

Of the ones who care

Why take advantage of who truly loves you?

Just care like you should

Especially in relationships

Don't talk about

Wanting someone faithful

If you are

Just going to be unfaithful.

I'll never understand

Why people get joy

Out of hurting other people

There should be nothing wrong

With being a good person

There shouldn't be such a thing

As being too nice

That just doesn't seem right.

It's time for a change

It's time to be proud of someone

Who cares for others

Cares about the well being

Of someone they don't even know

Be a good son/daughter

Be a good parent

Be a good friend

Be a good boyfriend/girlfriend

Believe it or not

Being nice to everyone

Is perfectly okay.

Don't be afraid

Don't be afraid

To speak out

Don't say something

Just because it's the popular thing to say

Be brave

Stand against the crowd

Going in the wrong direction

Be the leader

Of a new generation.

Lead a generation

Where we won't stand

For constant hate

Lead a generation

Where being nice and loving

Is what is okay.

Don't stand

With men/women that promote violence

Violence is never the right way

Battling violence

With more violence

And battling hate

With more hate

Will leave many of us

To never again awake.

This world needs peace

This world needs each one of us

In order

To make that happen

Can you imagine this world with less hate?

Exaggeration

People will

Exaggerate on stories

People will

Make up stories

People will do

Whatever it takes

To keep hate in the world.

Something isn't a problem

Until we are told

It's a problem.

When will we think for ourselves?

When will we love?

When will we all want peace?

Don't believe

Everything you see

Don't believe

Everything you are told

You are told

There is racism

But is there racism only against one race?

Absolutely not

There's racism

In every race

But you can't judge

An entire race

On the actions

Of one man's hate.

"Don't feed into the hate just because you are told to."

It doesn't take much

Open the door for someone

Smile

And ask how someone's doing

Let them know

Someone cares about them

Someone cares

Where they will be

Tomorrow

Next week

And five years from now.

Help out that man

That has hit rock bottom

Help out that man

That has nowhere to go

Nowhere to live

No one

Deserves to be homeless

We are willing

To help other societies

Before we help our own

Every place

In this world needs help

But before we help others

We must help ourselves.

We can't help

Change the world

Until we have changed

Everything here

It doesn't take much

To make a change

Not everyone

Will be able to help

In the same way

But do everything you possibly can

Because being a good person

Is the best thing

You can be in this world.

Homeless

You say you want to help

But do you really?

Don't tell everyone

When you help someone

That is homeless

Don't tell everyone

Just because you want everyone

To tell you

How good of a person you are

Don't tell everyone

Just because you crave attention.

Help

Because people need to be helped

Help

Because some people

Don't have anybody

Help

Because you want to see

A real change in the world.

Every homeless person

Has a different story

Some people

Can help the position they are in

Although

Many people cannot.

Simple things such as

Giving a man a meal

Giving a man some help

For a job position

Can truly change

The entire life

Of a man in dire need.

Let's stop the bleeding

Don't live life

With the eye for an eye strategy

Imagine just for a second

If it was your father/mother

Brother/sister

Boyfriend/girlfriend

Treat others

As you want to be treated.

Even if

Someone treats you wrong

Doesn't mean

You have to treat them

How they treated you

Let's stop the bleeding

Let's bring the crime rate down

Rape

Robbery

Murder

Let's change the world

And have

Less innocent lives ruined.

Forcing a lifestyle

We wouldn't want to have a world

Where everyone is the same

So don't expect

Someone to live

And believe in things

The same way that you do.

It's okay to live your lifestyle

However you please

Within reason of course

It's okay for you

To react differently

To be sad differently

To be happy differently.

What is not okay

Is you judging someone

For living

And believing differently

Than you do

We all don't have to agree

On how someone

Chooses to live

But guess what?

Their life

Is not your life to live.

You are not alone

Depression

Anxiety

Feeling like you are

Never good enough

Just know that you are loved.

I care

And I know

Many others do too

There are billions of people

In this world

But I really do

Care about each

And every one.

I never want to see someone

Contemplate

If life is worth living anymore

We only get to live once

So let's live it right

Let's try to

Stress less

And become

Whatever is our best.

Do what you love

Don't be unhappy

Don't hate your life

Be comfortable

Be happy

Love what you do.

Don't think from

A what if

Or how can I perspective

Do what you love

No matter what life

Throws in your direction.

Whether it's owning a business

Becoming a doctor

Becoming a teacher

Becoming a artist

Do whatever it takes

In order to make it happen

No excuses

No thinking about

What could have been.

Life will throw us obstacles

Where we will have to change

How we plan on

Making our dreams come true

But you can't give up

Never give up

Do whatever it is

That you love to do.

"Don't die while you're still alive."

Who protects you

Why talk down who protects you?

There should be respect

For the police and military

Are there people in uniform that make mistakes?

Of course so

They are human

Just like the rest of us

However

The overwhelming majority

Are in uniform

To help you stay free

They risk life every day

To help you live safely.

People that risk life for others

Should be who we look up too

Not someone

Who plays a sport

Sings

Or acts in movies

For millions of dollars.

We live in a society

Where we mourn the loss

Of a Hollywood star for weeks

But don't give any attention

To the man

That died to keep this country

The land of the free.

We will give the shirt off our back

To a celebrity in need

But walk right past a homeless veteran

That put his life on the line

For you and me.

It's time

Don't judge

An entire race

Or gender

Just because the actions

Of one individual.

There is good and bad

Of everyone

Every day

We are told to hate

Every day

We are told to separate

Let today

Be a new day.

It's time

Time for a change

Time to not judge

Just love.

Time to pick another man up

When everyone else

Just wants to keep him down

It's time

To make a difference

It's time

To love more

Hate less

And show some respect.

Don't wait until

Tomorrow

Next week

Or next year

Today is the time

Are you ready?

Because it's time…

God

The most important part of changing the world

Is having

God in our world

I realize

There are people that aren't religious

There are people

That don't believe

The same way I believe.

Just know however

He's the only one

Who doesn't judge

When times are great

He's there

When times are tough

He's there.

Having him in your life

Will take you to a place

You couldn't even dream of

Let everything go

And finally

Have a peace of mind.

Be able to become

Who

You were intended to become

In my past

I've made many mistakes

But God helped me overcome

And he can help you too

Get right with God

And let's change the world!

> *"Don't believe that you can't make a difference."*

> *"Together... we can all be free."*

Thank you,

Ryan Hamilton

35109856R00077

Made in the USA
Middletown, DE
04 February 2019